ANIMAL PUNS

ADULT COLORING BOOK

THESE AMOOSING PUNS WILL QUACK YOU UP!

I FIND THIS AMOOSING

Come join us and receive free images!

Stay updated on our new arrivals and download your free images.

www.motherdearestbooks.com/free

It is with great pleasure that we thank you for purchasing our adult coloring book. We find that there is nothing more relaxing than sitting down with a box of colored pencils and coloring beautiful images for hours. Whether you enjoy intricate patterns or ornately drawn animals we are certain you will be extremely pleased with the images inside this book. Please relax, clear your mind and color to your hearts content.

Enjoy!

Mother Dearest Coloring Books

An animal pun and adventure adventure Alpaca Anything!

THIS SONG IS A WAY I FIND. I FIND A WAY

Oh the Humanatee

What the mermaids - what do we have here!

Easy Peasy Beautiful Lover Squirrel

Flamingo

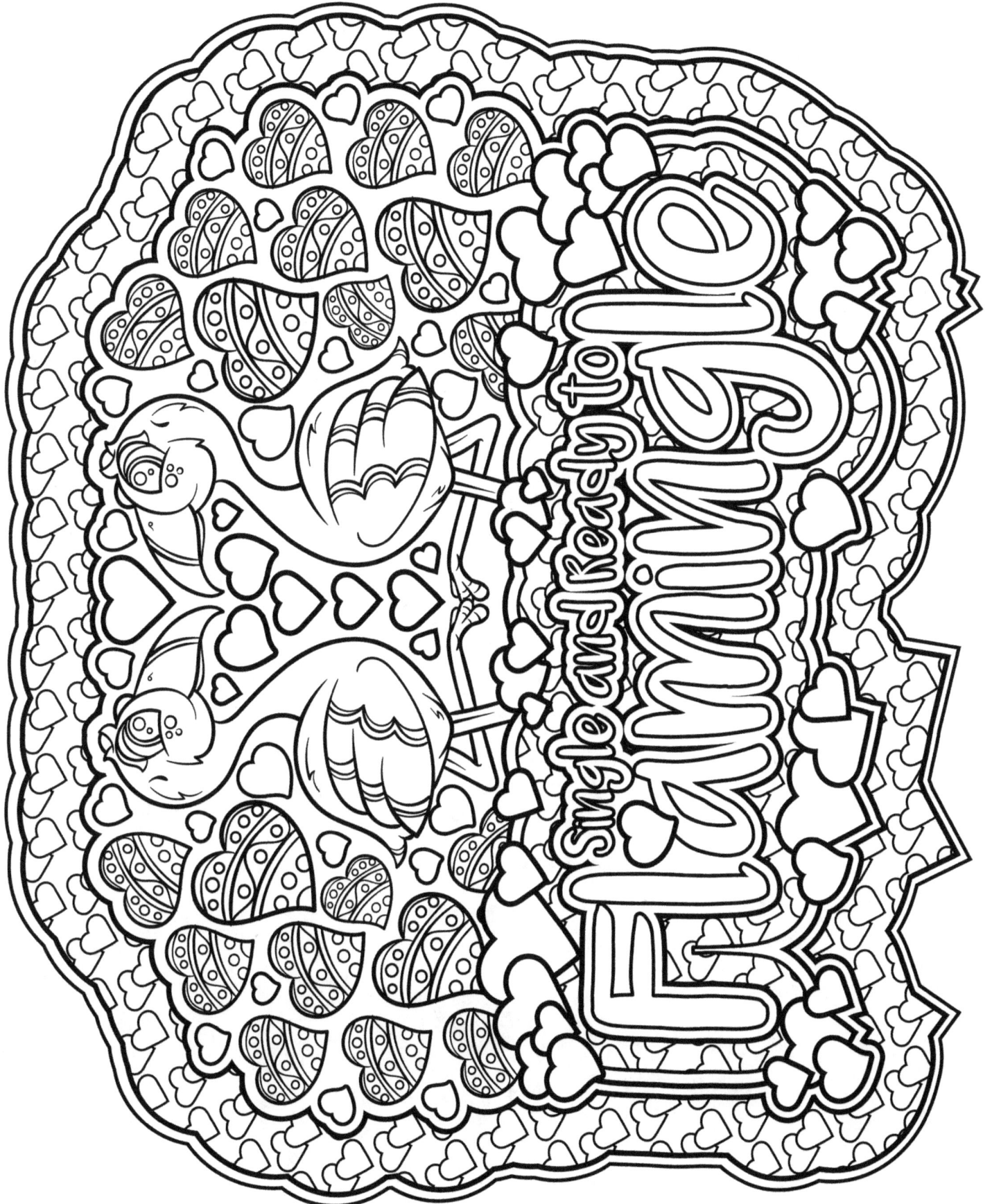

Single and Ready to

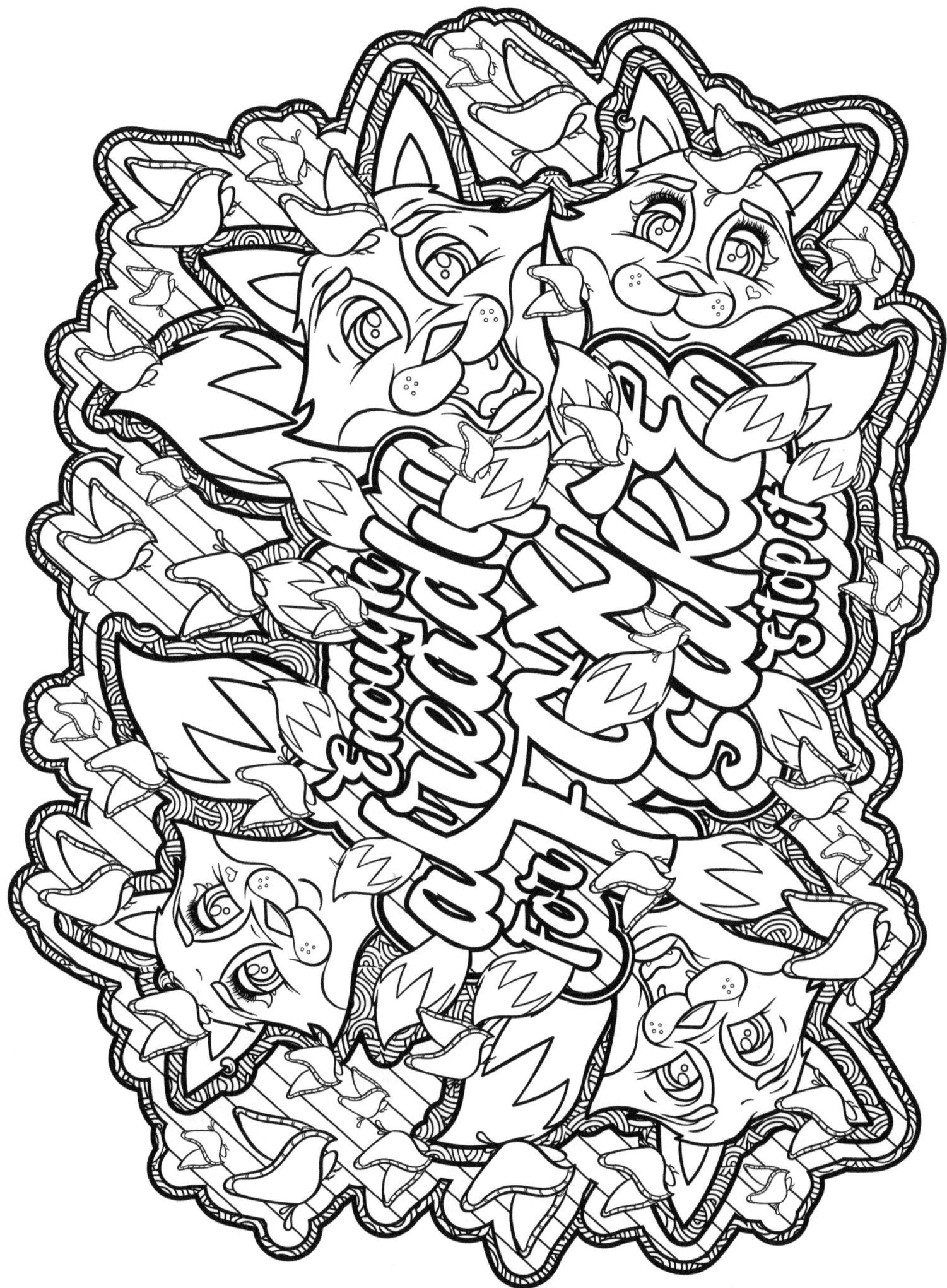

Well This is Awkward

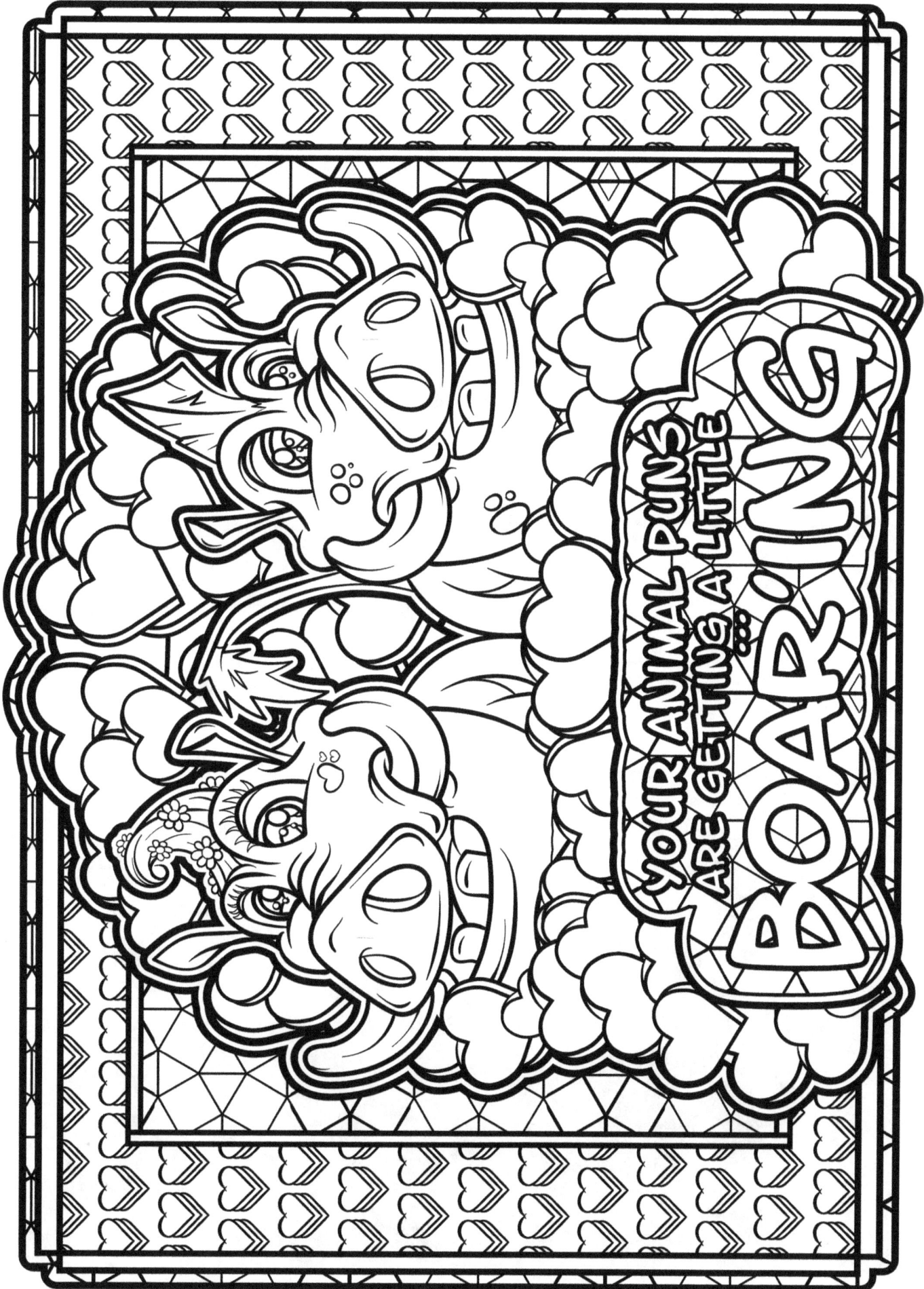

YOUR ANIMAL PUNS ARE GETTING A LITTLE... BOARING

Iguana but i have a Reptile dysfunction

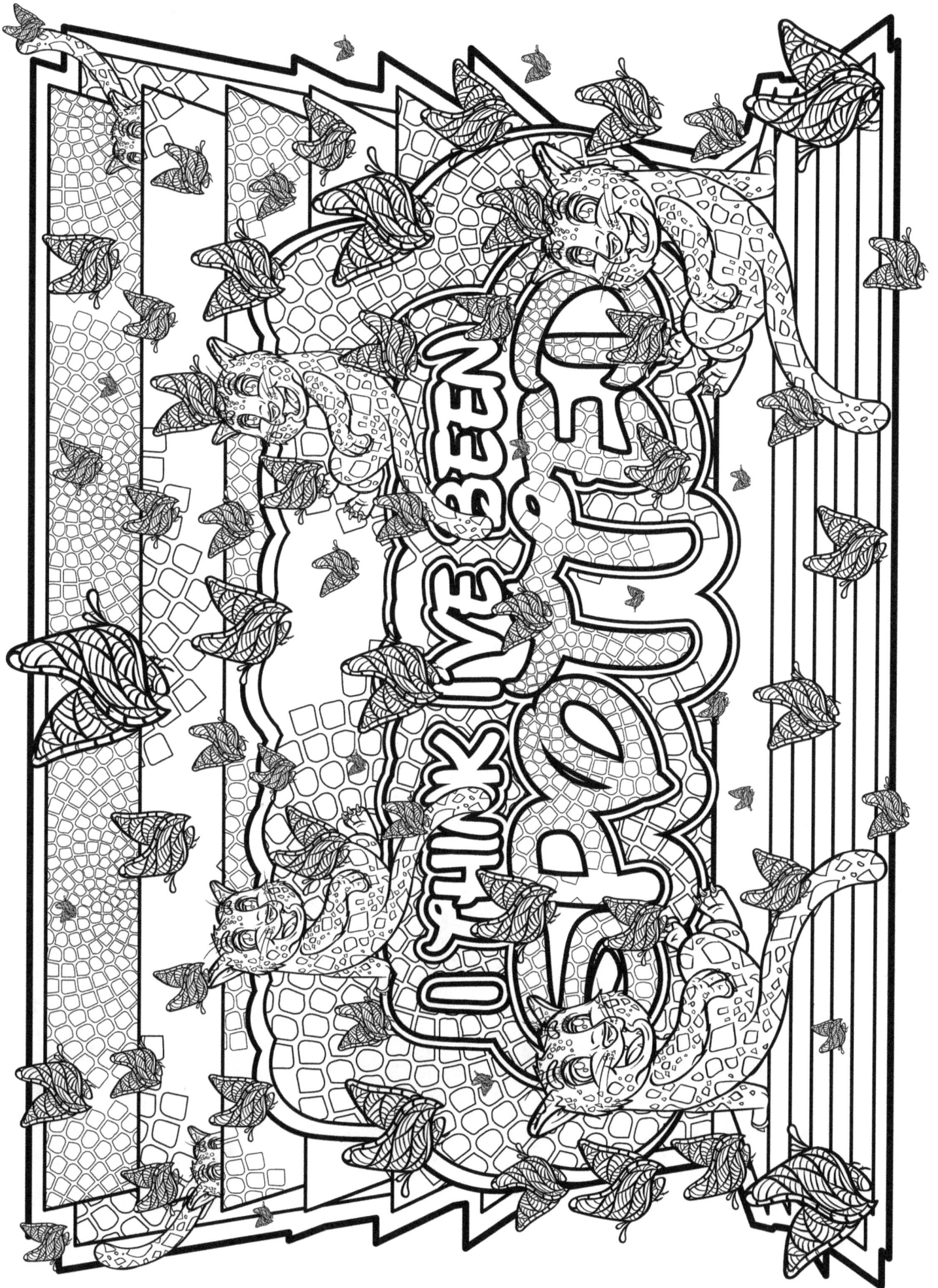
WHO WOULD'VE THINK YOU'D'VE BEEN

ARE YOU KITTEN ME RIGHT NOW?!

WHAT DO YOU MEAN... I'M NOT A BEAR?

I HAVE ALL THE KOALA-FICATIONS

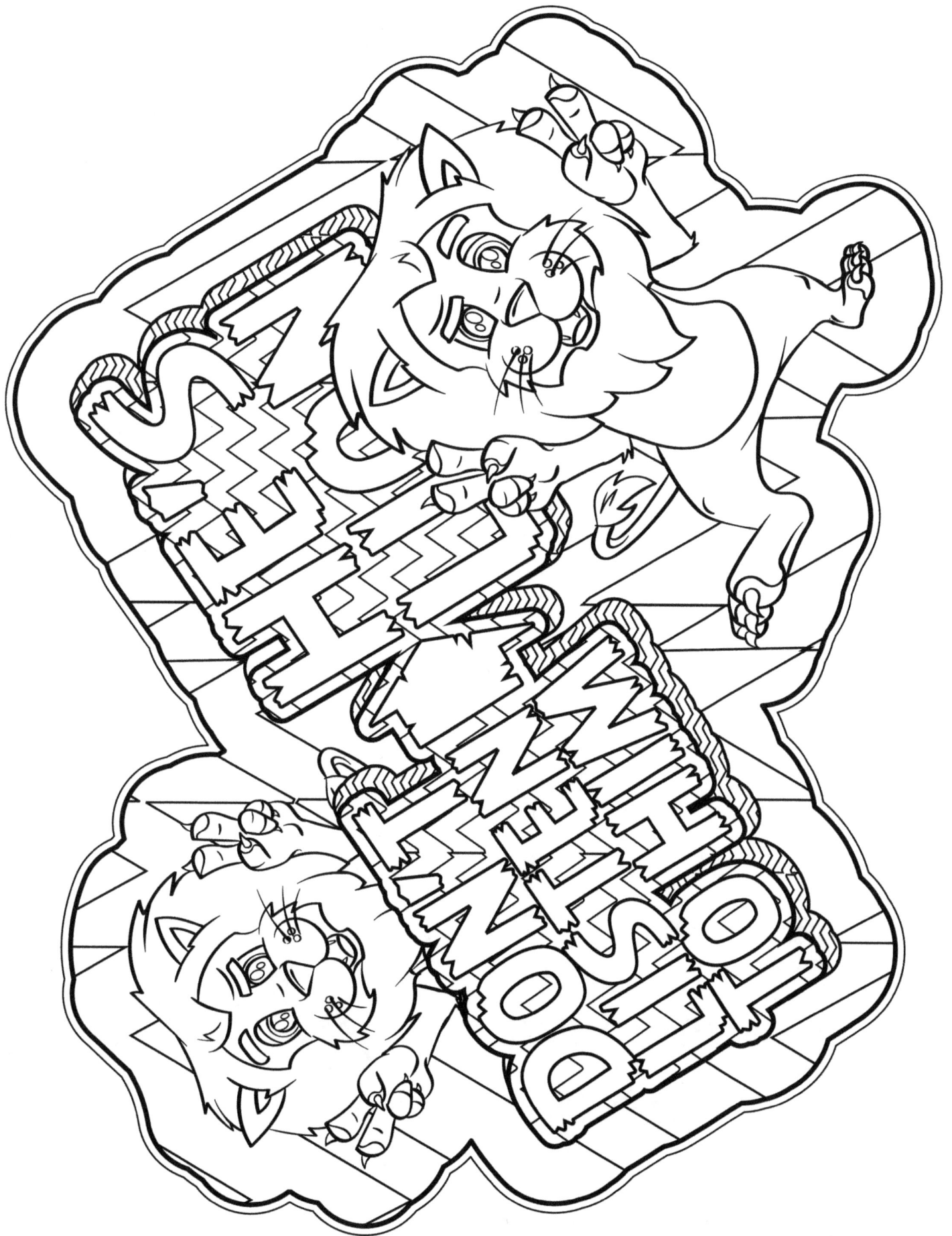

I'm a little horse!

Can I trouble you for a glass of water?

MOM SAYS I SPEND TOO MUCH TIME ON THE WEB

OWL ALWAYS LOVE YOU

This is PANDA*MONIUM

Stop Making Me Laugh you'll make me PISS SPARKS

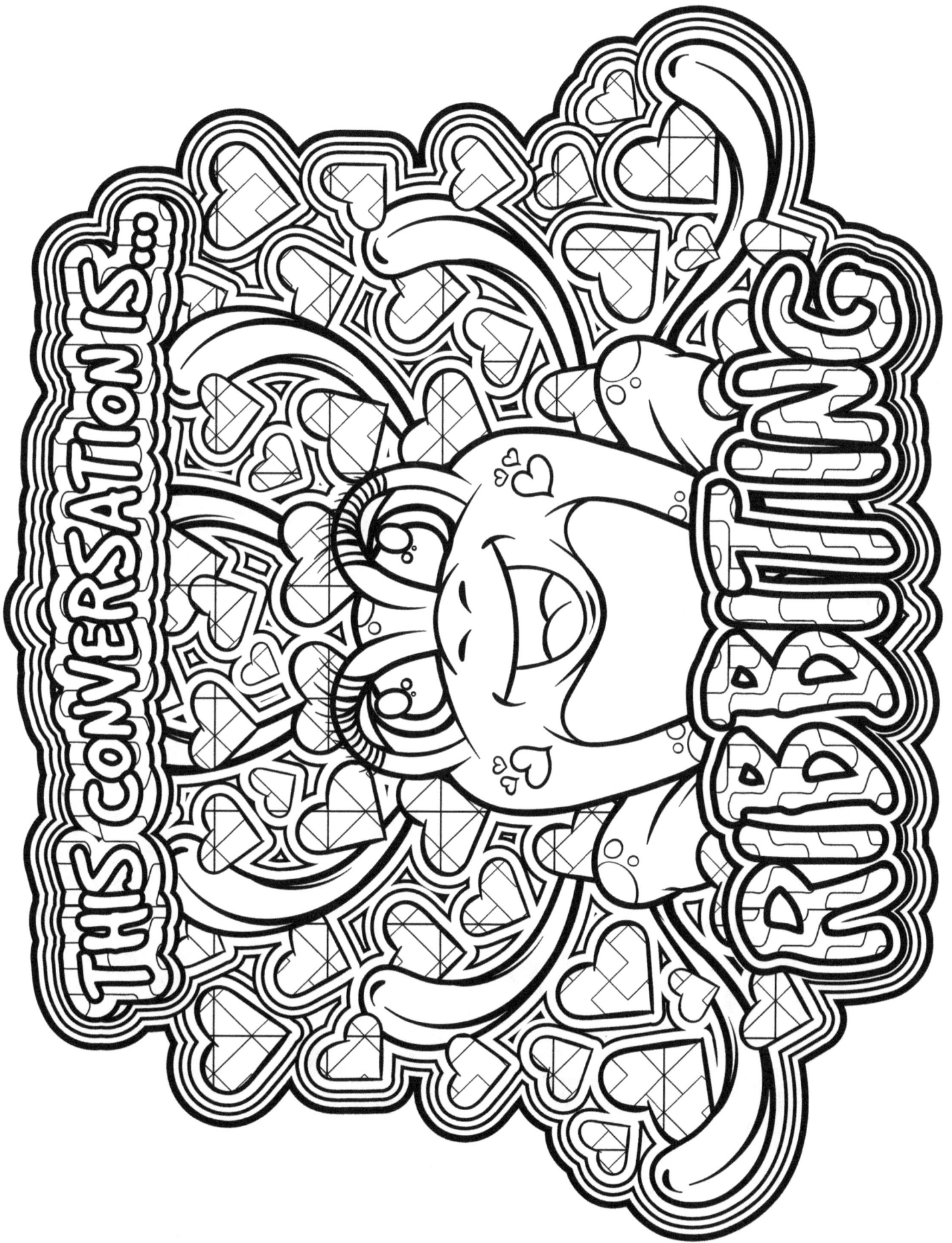

THIS CONVERSATION IS...

RIBBITING

STOP BEING SO TOXIC

WHY DON'T OYSTERS GIVE TO CHARITY?

Because they're Shellfish

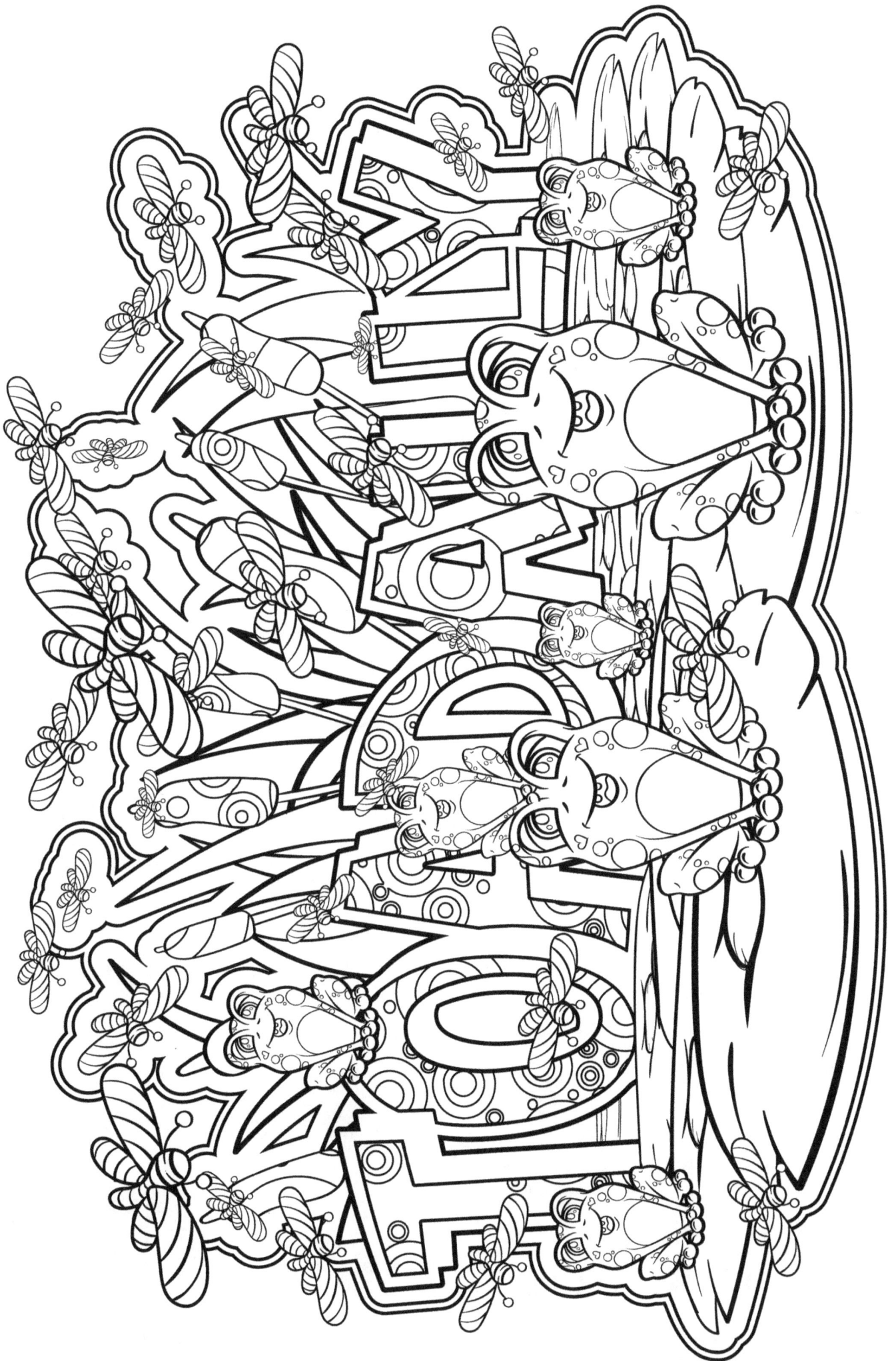

ANIMAL PUNS HUH? tOUCAN Play Well tHAT GAME

This Arguing is Becoming

www.ingramcontent.com/pod-product-compliance
Lightning Source LLC
Chambersburg PA
CBHW081650270326
41933CB00018B/3419